FLASHES OF GENIUS

Original title: Newton e la formula dell'antigravità

Texts and illustrations by Luca Novelli

Graphic design by Studio Link (www.studio-link.it)

Copyright © 2008 Luca Novelli/Quipos

Copyright © 2008 Editoriale Scienza S.r.l., Firenze –Trieste

www.editorialescienza.it

www.giunti.it

English edition published in the USA by

Chicago Review Press Incorporated

814 North Franklin Street

Chicago, Illinois 60610

ISBN 978-1-61373-861-0

Library of Congress Cataloging-in-Publication Data

Is available from the Library of Congress.

Printed in the United States of America

5 4 3 2 1

Luca Novelli

Newton
and the
Antigravity Formula

CHICAGO
REVIEW
PRESS

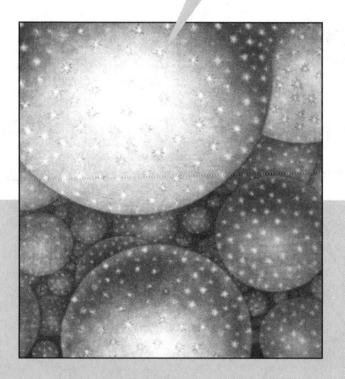

"Truth is ever to be found in simplicity, and not in the multiplicity and confusion of things."

Isaac Newton

Contents

Isaac Newton

"To myself I seem to have been only like a boy playing on the sea-shore, and diverting myself in now and then finding a smoother pebble or a prettier shell than ordinary, whilst the great ocean of truth lay all undiscovered before me."

Isaac Newton is the father of celestial mechanics.
He discovered the composite nature of light.
He's the creator of the mathematics used by all
the scientists who have come after him. It was
Isaac Newton who discovered the law of
universal gravitation, a law of physics that
everything and everyone, including the
planets and stars, must obey.

In this book, Isaac himself talks about his
life and his discoveries: from the prickly local boy
to the powerful adviser to kings and queens. His
story takes us to 17th-century England, a world
that, thanks to new and brilliant ideas like
Newton's, was slowly becoming more enlightened.

WHAT YOU'LL FIND IN THIS BOOK

There's me, Isaac Newton,
telling my story.

There's my childhood
and teenage years on the
Woolsthorpe farm, and
my arrival at the
University of Cambridge.

YOU'LL KEEP THE
PLACE CLEAN
AND POLISH OUR
BOOTS WHILE
YOU'RE
HERE.

PLOP!

There's the time of
the Black Death and
the true story about
the apple.

There are my studies about light, and the discovery of the law that describes the movement of the stars and planets.

There's my work at the Royal Mint of London and my brilliant career in the service of the kings and queens of England.

Lastly, there's a dictionary . . . a Gravitational Dictionary.

The World Awaiting Newton

It's a world where no man has ever left Earth's surface

The island of Manhattan (in New York) has recently been bought from the American Indians.

England is torn by civil and religious wars.

Heretics are burned alive in the square.

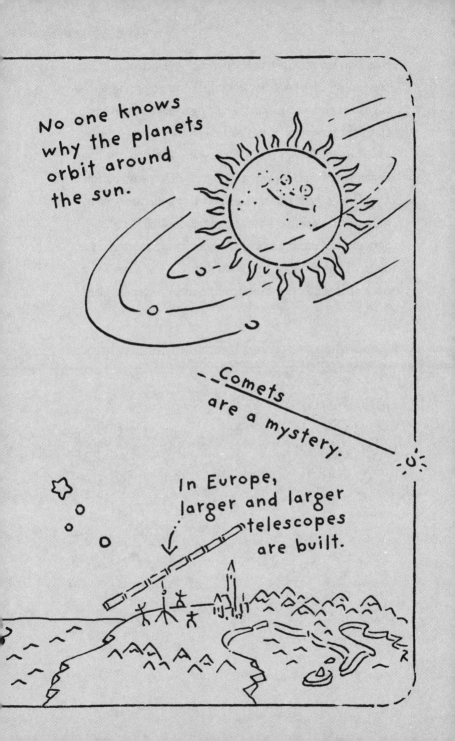

Isaac Newton was born in Woolsthorpe in Lincolnshire, England, on Christmas Day 1642. That was according to the English calendar that was then being used, while on the European continent it was already January 4, 1643.

The year 1642 is tragic for England. It marks the beginning of a civil war that will end with the execution of King Charles I and the establishment of a dictatorship by his rival, the puritan Oliver Cromwell. England is still an agricultural country, where the nobility are masters of much of the country, and ownership of a few acres and a flock of sheep is already a sign of a certain social status.

1. Me, Isaac Newton

Welcome to Woolsthorpe and my dad's house. It's a white building surrounded by fields and pastures that are part of the farm. I come from a family of wealthy farmers. For over a hundred years, we Newtons have plowed the earth and expanded our estate in Lincolnshire.

GREAT TO SEE YOU, MY FRIENDS OF THE UNIVERSE!

Woolsthorpe

My dad's name was Isaac as well. I never knew him because he died before I was born. Basically, I was born an orphan. My mom, Hannah, is no longer at home, either. She's remarried. And she went to live with her new husband. I really miss her. And I also miss having a dad.

In Woolsthorpe, I live with my grandmother and I could have plenty of company. My great-grandfather had seven children. My grandfather Robert had eleven. So a small army of uncles, aunts, and cousins live nearby. But I don't go looking for them, and they don't come looking for me. I almost always play alone on the farm, and there's so much to discover. There are dozens of cattle and more than 200 farm animals, yard animals, horses, the orchard, the canals . . .

CAN YOU BELIEVE THAT HE'LL BECOME ONE OF THE GREATEST GENIUSES OF ALL TIME?

Sometimes I climb up the highest hill and sit and look at the horizon. The valley is dotted with villages and the sea is 20 miles (32 km) to the east—the large arm of the Atlantic Ocean called the North Sea. Sometimes I can smell the sea on the wind. And there's so much wind here in Lincolnshire.

My dad couldn't read or write. He signed his will with an X. His brother and many other Newtons are illiterate. However, his mother, Hannah Ayscough, was the daughter of a gentleman. His brother William graduated in literature from the University of Cambridge. Now he's a reverend in a nearby village.

Uncle William has many books that smell old in his rectory. Most of them are heavy church books, but not all of them. They're interesting. Maybe they hold the answers to the many questions I have.

How Does the Universe Work?

Before Isaac was born, there were some revolutionary theories about this. For example, Copernicus and Kepler argued that the Earth revolves around the sun and not the other way around, which doesn't seem right when you look at the rising and setting of the sun. They also said that every day the Earth rotates on its axis at a crazy speed. But then why don't we fly off, instead of our feet remaining firmly on the ground?

By suggesting the idea of the Earth's motion, Galileo Galilei risked torture and the death penalty. By Newton's day this truth is accepted by wise men across the globe. But still nobody could explain what laws governed the great dance of the planets, comets, and whatever else is up there in the sky.

2. I Have a Terrible Temper

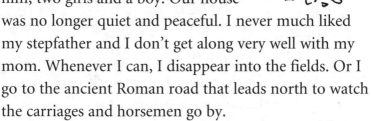

My stepfather has died and my mom has returned to live at Woolsthorpe. She brought with her three children she had with him, two girls and a boy. Our house was no longer quiet and peaceful. I never much liked my stepfather and I don't get along very well with my mom. Whenever I can, I disappear into the fields. Or I go to the ancient Roman road that leads north to watch the carriages and horsemen go by.

In short, Woolsthorpe is beginning to feel too small. So, when I am 12 years old, I am very happy when my mom decides to send me to school in Grantham, the nearest village. I live with Mr. Clark, the pharmacist.

I really like his
workshop and
especially his
lab. But there
are many things
I don't like in
Grantham. At
school they put
me on the last

bench, with the worst of the class. In fact, at
Woolsthorpe I'd only received a very basic education.
And I'm often the butt of the jokes of Mr. Clark's
stepchildren, Edward and Arthur.

I ended up in a fistfight with Arthur. I beat him and
wanted to stop because I find fighting stupid. But he
accused me of being a coward and then pushed me
against the wall, hurting my nose. So I grabbed him by
the ears and did the same to him, banging his face
against the wall.

ONCE IT'S DONE, IT'S DONE!

I don't even mix with the other boys. But I can count on one good friend, the pharmacist's stepdaughter. She is nice and kind. I'm happy when I am with her, and she's happy with me. I make wooden things for her, like furniture for her dolls and funny models, like a cart that I can move by turning a crank. I even build a small windmill, similar to the one they are building north of the city. I went to see it and copied the design.

I even invented a lantern . . . a foldable one made of paper. You turn it off during the day, and fold it and keep it inside a book. Sometimes, on moonless nights, I attach it to the tail of a kite and fly it over the houses, scaring the inhabitants of Grantham. They've never seen anything fly in their lives, except birds. Luckily I don't set fire to the city. The Puritans would have put me in the pillory at the very least for a stunt like that.

This stern knight is Oliver Cromwell. While the young Isaac has fun building paper lanterns, Oliver Cromwell has appointed himself the Lord Protector of England. In this office he can dissolve and convene Parliament at will. Under his dictatorship, battles and massacres are commonplace. He has subdued Ireland and Scotland and has declared war on Holland and Spain.

Cromwell is a Puritan, and the Puritans support him. They're Protestant Christians and strict enforcers of mandatory virtue, even to the point of banning festivities and amusements in towns and villages. Under Cromwell's rule, most Britons miss the previous king, Charles I.

3. Boring and Interesting Subjects

At King's School in Grantham I make progress.
Gradually I move forward through the benches in front
of me until I get to the first one, reserved for the best in
the class. I scratch my name onto each bench that I sit
at. Isaac Newton, Isaac Newton. . . . I know, you're not
supposed to do it, but my name, which I etched into a
windowsill, is considered a historical find in your time.

The subjects that I have to study aren't exciting:
Latin, English grammar, and Bible commentary.
Nothing else. Groan. Outside of school I'm considered
"weird." I make sundials everywhere, and I can tell you
the exact time just by looking at my shadow.

One terribly windy day, which everyone remembers for the death of Cromwell, the great dictator, I carry out an odd experiment. I prove that by jumping in the same direction as the wind, my jumps are longer. It's my first contact with the forces of motion.

I very happily draw with charcoal, not only on paper but also on the walls of the house where I'm staying. I even did a portrait of the former King Charles I. But Mr. Clark has had enough of my graffiti.

When school is over I return to the farm. My mom wants me to look after it. But when I am given a job, I get lost. If they give me sheep to watch, I let them stray into the neighbors' fields.

If they send me to the market, I always forget what I should be selling or buying. I always have a few books with me. And I even forget to eat, something inconceivable in these times of hunger and scarcity.

No, I'm not made for the countryside. Instead, I choose a different life. My uncle William and my teacher Stokes support me in my choice. Even the servant to whom my mom entrusted me is very happy when I tell him that I am leaving and says it is the right decision because I am only fit for college.

At the school in Grantham, Isaac learns only one thing well: Latin. He reads, writes, and speaks it. The Latin spoken by the ancient Romans in Europe is a dead language these days, replaced by a variety of national languages, but in the 17th century it's still used by educated people. It makes it possible to avoid misunderstandings due to the differences in national languages, and allows new ideas to spread more quickly. It is in fact the language of scientists, just as today English is used across the world.

Kepler's and Galileo's works were translated and spread in Latin. Almost all the books Isaac reads are in Latin, and it's with this language that he goes to conquer the University of Cambridge.

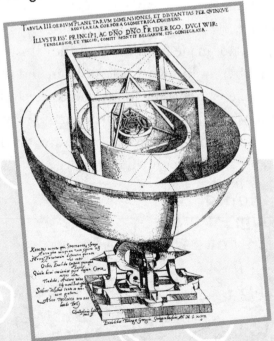

4. Discovering Cambridge

I'm 19 when, on June 4, 1661, I enter Trinity, the most famous college in Cambridge, part of the most prestigious university in England. Part of the University of Oxford, today it's more popular and more powerful than its older relative.

When I arrive, Cambridge is little more than a village full of taverns for students. The village still has a medieval look, but the chapel and colleges lined up on the banks of the River Cam are impressive. There are many schools, and they are huge, serious, and inspire awe.

WELCOME TO CAMBRIDGE, YOUNG MAN.

THE KING'S COLLEGE CHAPEL

THE RIVER CAM

I take entrance tests at Trinity College and am admitted to the school. I had to buy a lock for the desk, a bottle of ink, a notebook, a pound of candles, and . . . a chamber pot. Of course, that is because toilets, like computers, were still a long way from being invented in my time.

NOTEBOOK QUILL INK CHAMBER POT CANDLES

A month later, along with 16 other students, I am sworn in to the university. I solemnly promise to defend the honor of this institution. Whoever attends Cambridge receives academic titles that will enable him to have a successful public or religious career. But I don't attend it for those reasons, even if I will spend almost 27 years of my life there.

WELCOME TO TRINITY COLLEGE

So far I have told you the best part about my arrival in Cambridge. The rest of it embarrasses me a bit. Despite being the heir to a considerable fortune, I enter Trinity College as a *subsizar*—a student who must earn his way by doing grunt work for teachers and *pensioners*, who are well-off students who pay higher fees. The sons of nobles, baronets, or knights, all pensioners, mustn't serve others during meals, nor clean their shoes, nor empty the chamber pots of the lecturers and fellow students into the river.

I'm not the only subsizar at Trinity College. There are more than a dozen of us, but this situation really bothers me. It doesn't seem right, neither for me nor for anyone else. It reflects the class divisions that still face the society of England. It's a reality that I have to deal with.

Here's the Frenchman René Descartes: philosopher, mathematician, physicist. He died in 1650, but he started a school of thought that considers all the things in the sky and on earth as parts in a complex system of mechanisms that can be mathematically and geometrically described. At the University of Cambridge, the young Newton discovers this philosophy of nature called "mechanistic." He also discovers a revolution taking place in the sciences based on astronomy, optics, and mechanics. Isaac eagerly follows this revolution and the thinking of Descartes. Then, as with all geniuses, he surpasses the masters.

5. Student Life

I don't allow myself many luxuries. Sometimes I buy cherries, jelly, cream, and some wine. I spend almost all my money on books and a lot on clothing. I don't want to look like a subsizar. I don't go to the taverns and other places in the city very much, not just because the rules of the university officially forbid it, but because I have few friends with whom to enjoy a night on the town.

There are plenty of attractions in town for layabouts in addition to all the taverns. Not far from the college and in the space of just a few days, a man who'd killed his wife was hanged, a bank robber was grilled and questioned literally to death, and an attorney was pilloried on Peas Hill, the main street in Cambridge. On these occasions, a large screaming and hateful crowd gathers around the unfortunate person. There are even those who mock the victims, even as they're about to die.

I study a lot, but without following the professors' advice. The classes at Cambridge are, in fact, still medieval: rhetoric, Greek, more Latin,

and lots and lots of Aristotle. In practice, I only flip through certain books, and as soon as I understand what the tutor wants to hear during the exams, I put them aside and I start to read books that are more interesting . . . like those of Descartes, Galileo, or Robert Boyle, the author of *The Sceptical Chymist*. It doesn't always work; at the exam for a scholarship they ask me things I don't know and I flunk the test.

ORIGINAL DRAWING BY NEWTON

HERE'S ONE OF MY MACHINES!

Meanwhile I'm interested in perpetual motion. I'd like to know what matter and light are made of, what is time, and why the planets orbit around the sun. In short, I want to become a philosopher of nature, or a lover of knowledge, in the truest sense of the word.

In 1665 I take the last exams and I receive my degree. I get it without any particular honors and without any enthusiasm. Indeed, I wanted to immediately start a master's degree, or a postgraduate course, but Cambridge is about to be overwhelmed by a national tragedy that will change many things.

THE PLAGUE! THE PLAGUE!

Of all the great misfortunes that can affect a country, the worst by far is the Black Plague. It's called that because of the dark lumps that appear on the body of the sick, who then die in horrific pain. It's caused by a microbe (*Yersinia pestis*) that is transmitted by rat fleas, which also bite humans. The best prevention methods are cleanliness and good hygiene, which are rare in 17th-century Europe. Even in Cambridge there are neither bathrooms nor sewers, and people rarely wash. At the time of Newton, there is no known cure for the plague.

Thousands of people abandon the cities by any means possible. The funerals of plague victims are preceded by a man who rings a bell. But real funerals are few and far between. The number of dead are in the thousands; they are collected and piled onto pushcarts and buried in mass graves.

AAAAAAAH!

6. The Days of the Black Death

It wasn't a good winter. The Thames froze twice. Then, as soon as the temperature grew milder, the Great Plague struck England once more. The plague of 10 years ago claimed more than 100,000 victims, almost all of them in the big cities.

When the plague rages, only one place is safe, and that is an isolated house in the countryside. I should stay in Cambridge to earn a master's degree, but the university empties and so I return to Woolsthorpe, hoping that the wind will dispel the fogs of the disease.

It'll be a happy day when someone finds out what causes it. For now, bonfires are lit and smelling herbs are burned in the streets. Dogs and cats are blamed. They are captured and killed at the expense of the state. But it's no use. In fact, it's worse. In London 7,000 die in a single week. It's terrible.

I end up staying in Woolsthorpe for nearly 18 months. The plague spares us. I don't mind being back home. I think and work on some extraordinary ideas. It'll be the most inventive period of my life. For a start, I create my own personal method of mathematics, which today is called differential and integral calculus.

Then, in my room, with a prism I bought at the market, I divide and then recreate a ray of light. It's the first step toward a new and original theory of light and color.

Finally an apple—the most famous apple in the universe—falls beside me.

For some time I've been wondering what gravity is. I look at the apple and the moon.

I'm beginning to think that the mysterious force that attracts the apple—and not just the apple— toward the center of the Earth is not a property that's limited to our planet. I think it may be extended to the moon, the solar system . . . and the entire universe.

For the young Newton, the years 1665 and 1666 are perhaps the most inventive. They're defined his "wonder years," that is, the most extraordinary years of his life as a scientist.

For England they're terrible years. After months and months of the plague, in September 1666 an uncontrollable fire destroys London. It burns the harbor and the theatre districts, it burns mansions and hovels. Thirteen thousand houses and 80 churches are destroyed. It's the greatest disaster in British history.

But with the fire the plague ends, and the capital is rebuilt more beautiful than before.

7. The Ghost of Light

I bought my first prism at a local fair. It was little more than a piece of glass cut into a triangular shape. After that, I built my own prisms by cutting and grinding glass fragments. Looking through a prism the world seems to rotate, through well-known phenomenon called refraction. But if a prism is struck with a particular beam of light, you get an unexpected result.

I created a light beam by making a small hole in a closed window shutter and making my room dark. The result is that the prism projects a strip of colors that always happen in the same order: red, orange, yellow, green, blue, indigo, and violet. I called it a "spectrum," because normally it is invisible, like ghosts.

BLUE
GREEN
YELLOW
RED

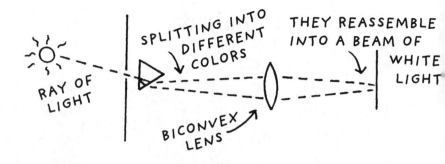

RAY OF LIGHT

SPLITTING INTO DIFFERENT COLORS

THEY REASSEMBLE INTO A BEAM OF WHITE LIGHT

BICONVEX LENS

Using the prism, I split white light into its component colors. Using other prisms, I can reassemble these components back into a beam of white light, or separate them further into single-color beams. Even if I've called it a spectrum, this set of colors is the reality of white light, which—I'll claim—is perhaps made of different "particles."

When I reveal this discovery, I make the great Dutch physicist Christiaan Huygens angry. He says that "they can't be particles because when the light rays meet, they don't get displaced, like particles would be. I think they're waves, like sound waves."

SO... WHAT IS LIGHT?

I'm only a young graduate. He's the greatest physicist in Europe. Yet my "corpuscular" (particle) hypothesis will have the upper hand for nearly two centuries. In the end we'll discover that, surprisingly, we're both right.

Light consists of particles—photons—that behave like waves . . . but how and why will not be shown until many, many years later.

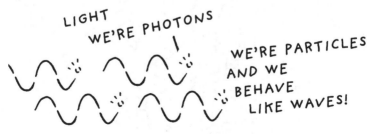

I'M A VERY DELICATE ORGAN!

In the enthusiasm of his research on light, Newton also does some very silly things. One time, he fixed one eye on the sun until he nearly ruined his eyesight. Another time, in trying to alter the curve of the retina to see the effect it created, he placed a thin needle "between the eye and the bone," risking an infection and blindness.

ISAAC! ARE YOU SURE YOU'RE A GENIUS?

8. A Young Man with a Career

The Black Death is over. The university is again filled with students and teachers. The atmosphere is more relaxed in the colleges, some say too much. Even my attitude is somewhat improved, maybe because I'm glad to have survived, unlike tens of thousands of my countrymen. So I celebrate graduation by throwing a party, and I spend a lot of money on clothes and taverns.

I've decided: I'll follow a career at Cambridge. In 1667 I become a minor fellow, nine months later a major fellow, and in 1668 I become a Master of Arts.

It's a stable career and I have a fixed salary. I'm supposed to also take the Anglican Church holy orders and pledge allegiance to this religion, which is something I try to avoid because my ideas in this regard aren't exactly orthodox.

Other than that, I could just laze about at Cambridge, like most of my colleagues do and whose main activities are . . .

It's a wild and carefree period for universities and colleges, but this allows me to do the research that I want to do in complete freedom.

I even manage to install an entire alchemic laboratory in my room, with a furnace, flasks, and burners. It looks like a magician's cave.

I even prepare my own medicine here. There are generic cures for the plague, measles, and smallpox, made with recipes that today could kill a horse. But I don't believe in the paranormal, black magic, or other such things.

THERE ARE LOTS OF THINGS TO SEE UP THERE!

Here is Galileo Galilei. He was the first astronomer to use a telescope to observe the moon and other celestial objects. After him, many others have observed the sky with this instrument, but the views were always hampered by smudges of color.

Newton solves the problem. His studies of the nature of light, together with his skills at building with his hands, enable him to build a more sophisticated instrument: a telescope without color bluriness.

BRAVO... NEWTON!

9. Problems as a Professor

I received an unexpected honor. The math chair Isaac Barrow left his professorship for a higher position and appointed me as his replacement. Professor Barrow will go down in history for having realized that I'm better than him. But I have a confession to make: my math classes are not very packed. Sometimes I find my classroom empty, and I return to my room grumbling.

Maybe my calculation methods are too modern for my students. But that just means I have more time for my research. I design and build a new telescope in my lab and send one to the Royal

Society in London, who greatly appreciate the gesture and the instrument. I'm officially an inventor.

The Royal Society promotes science and research in England. So, along with the telescope, I sent a report on my discoveries about the diffraction of light. And I regret it. Others immediately took credit for my discovery.

Meanwhile, the time to swear an oath to the state religion is approaching. All teachers must do it. For some time now I've been studying the history of religions, and I've found out many things that my fellow teachers wouldn't agree with.

It's one of my secrets. To read the ancient texts, I've studied very old languages to the point of becoming an expert on the Apocalypse, Noah, and the ancient kingdoms before the great flood.

My ideas—if they were disclosed—would land me in the stocks and lead to my expulsion from the university. Or—something that repels me—I'd have to lie. Luckily, I manage to get a royal exemption. I sigh with relief.

In 1679 my mom, Hannah, gets sick. I return to Woolsthorpe where I look after her with affection. But it's hopeless. She dies in June 1679. It's a definitive break from my past.

In the winter of 1680–81 a comet appears in the skies over England. Comets arrive unexpectedly and are believed to predict famine, war, and disease, which are all pretty common in 17th-century Europe. Even the plague of 1665 had been "predicted" by a comet. But this particular celestial body instead heralds two big events for Newton: a young friend who will become famous and a new idea, as extraordinary as the universe.

10. Surprises in the Sky and Earth

The comet is huge. It appeared over the sky of Cambridge on December 12, 1680, disquieting and mysterious, with a tail as long as the King's College chapel. It remains visible for several months.

The comet's trajectory shows a strange "curved" trend, even seeming to rotate around the sun. John Flamsteed, the king's astronomer, pointed it out to me. His job is to observe and make a note of the stars at the Greenwich Observatory. His observations are particularly useful to seamen, but no one, not even Flamsteed himself, believes that they can be used to discover new laws about the universe.

In the meantime, my colleague Hooke writes an essay in which he proposes that all celestial bodies have an attraction or gravitational force toward their centers. He proposes, and I think.

Then a young man named Edmond Halley came to see me in Cambridge. He has recently become the secretary of the Royal Society and he studies comets. He asked me a series of questions.

I promise him some more precise answers. So I start to write and draw . . .

If comets follow ellipses just like the planets, even if much more elongated, then they also obey the same laws as the planets. So, little by little, sheet by sheet, a great idea takes shape in my notebook: the planets, the sun, and all the bodies in the universe influence each other due to the same law . . .

It is the Law of Universal Gravitation.

THE COMETS?

SOMETIMES THEY COME BACK . . . IN FACT, THEY ALWAYS DO!

This gentleman in a wig is Edmond Halley in old age. His father was a salt merchant. Halley will become one of the most famous astronomers in history. By studying comets of the past, he has discovered a great truth: sooner or later, all of them return to the solar system. Thanks to Newton's laws, Halley will foresee the return, after 75 years, of a comet seen in 1682. The prediction will come true and the comet will be named after him.

HERE'S HALLEY'S COMET!

WHAT DID I TELL YOU?

11. One Law, or Rather, Three

What I've discovered is too important. I must spread my idea, and at the same time protect it. So I publish a book where I lay out my whole theory. It has a very serious title: *Mathematical Principles of Natural Philosophy*. It includes all phenomena of celestial motion, arguing that the gravitational pull between the sun and the planets decreases with the square of the distance.

As soon as Hooke hears about the book, he wants credit. He claims that the idea of the square of the distance is his. In reality, he never wrote the formula. And in any case—this is what I say—he's a cheat and an imposter.

HERE'S "MY" LAW AND . . . A LOT MORE!

PHILOSOPHIÆ
NATURALIS
PRINCIPIA
MATHEMATICA

Autore JS. NEWTON, Trin. Coll. Cantab. Soc. Mathefeos Profeſſore Lucaſiano, & Societatis Regalis Sodali.

IMPRIMATUR·
S. PEPYS, Reg. Soc. PRÆSES.
Julii 5. 1686.

LONDINI,

Juſſu Societatis Regiæ ac Typis Joſephi Streater. Proſtat apud plures Bibliopolas. Anno MDCLXXXVII.

I WANT TO BE CITED!

GRRRR!

Hooke

Newton

My theory of gravitation is absolute; it applies to everything and everyone, not just the planets. Here are the most important things that it contains:

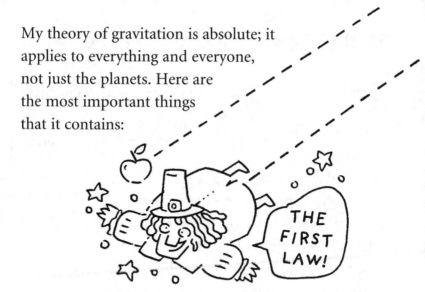

"An object at rest stays at rest and an object in motion stays in motion with the same speed and in the same direction unless acted upon by an unbalanced force."

The apple and I could stay in this state indefinitely, if no one gives us a little push. Our state also changes if we come close to a planet because it attracts us, and we'd start by going into orbit, and in the end land on its surface.

I even invented a new adjective: *centripetal*, that is "attraction toward the center." Every celestial body—and not only celestial—attracts other bodies toward its center.

THE SECOND LAW!

OUCH!

THWACK!

"The acceleration of an object depends directly upon the net force acting upon it."

As the force acting upon an object is increased, so the acceleration of the object is increased. The greater the mass of an object and the closer we are to its center, the more we are attracted to it.

THE THIRD LAW

WHAT ARE YOU DOING? ARE YOU PUSHING?

YOU'RE PUSHING!

"For every action, there is an equal and opposite reaction."

If we push a mass with a given force, it resists with an equal and opposite force. We can move it when our force exceeds that of the mass. The Earth attracts the moon, and the moon exerts an equal and opposing force on the Earth. This force can be visibly seen on the oceans, through the phenomenon of the tides.

Today the fact that the law of gravitation is universal doesn't surprise anyone. It's normal to think that the laws of physics and chemistry are valid both on Earth and on the furthermost planet in the galaxy. But that's not how it is in Newton's time, where the idea of the universe is still associated with ancient Greek cosmology, as well as the teachings of church leaders, such as St. Augustin. For them the sky was something that was far away and perfect, subject to angelic and divine laws, which were very different from those on Earth.

Instead, Newton says that "the law is equal for all," in heaven and on Earth, including for the seas and oceans.

12. Lunar Attraction

Among the Earthly wonders that can be explained using my theory, there are some practical ones that no one before me had managed to explain.

> EVEN THE WATERS OF THE OCEANS OBEY MY LAWS!

These include the tides, the daily rise and fall of the sea level along the coastlines. For sailors—especially those who sail the great oceans—understanding the nature of this phenomenon is very important. It's possible to anchor the ship several feet above the sea bed, only to find it beached just a few hours later. And vice versa.

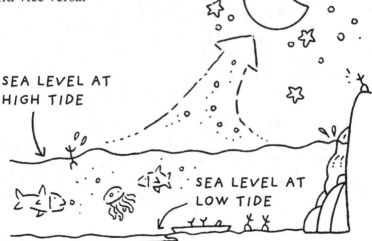

SEA LEVEL AT
HIGH TIDE

SEA LEVEL AT
LOW TIDE

Even Descartes and Galileo had been mistaken about what causes the tides. They couldn't accept the idea that the moon and the sun could cause an effect "at a distance." Some ancient philosophers had been closer to the truth.

My law gives a reasonable explanation: the tides are caused by the combined gravitational action of the moon and, to a lesser degree, the sun, and by the centrifugal force of the Earth.

The result is that across the planet there are two tides, with a 6 hour and 12 minute break between high tide and low tide. In some seas of the world, the difference in water level between high and low tide is as much as 50 feet (15 meters).

Among the many things explained by Newton's laws, one concerns a reality that we have to constantly deal with: the weight of things. Before Newton, few scientists and philosophers had dealt with this concept. Certainly objects have been weighed for centuries, with more or less accurate scales and with different measurement systems. But the first to define the nature of weight is Isaac Newton.

13. An Almost Magical Law

Of course. My law explains the weight of things.

Weight is nothing more than the measure of the force that draws us toward the center of the Earth.

That is, gravitational force. If you were on the moon, your weight would depend on its gravitational force, which is weaker.

It's not just the Earth that draws us toward its center. All bodies in the universe attract each other: the planets and the sun, the stars and the comets. They all obey the law that I discovered, which can be summed up with a formula.

My formula says that the force (F) that attracts two bodies to each other is proportional to their masses—quantity of matter—(M1 and M2) and inversely proportional to the squared distance between their centers (R2). G is a constant number that is equal throughout the universe.

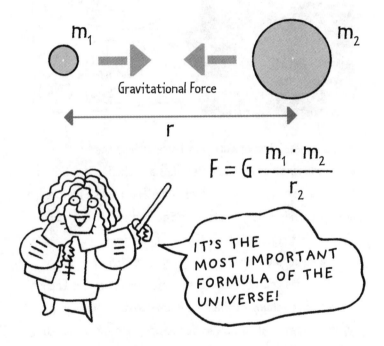

Gravitational Force

$$F = G \frac{m_1 \cdot m_2}{r_2}$$

IT'S THE MOST IMPORTANT FORMULA OF THE UNIVERSE!

In my time, the idea of this universal force seems magical or even divine, like a sign of God's active presence in the world.

All I can say is that my formula works, and it'll work wherever you go in the universe.

THE UNIVERSITY PRODUCES KNOWLEDGE!

KNOWLEDGE IS POWER!

I WANT TO HAVE POWER OVER THE UNIVERSITY!

Here's James II, the new king of England. He's the brother of Charles II, who has recently died. He's a Catholic, or rather a Christian loyal to the Church of Rome. Few English people are anymore. They're loyal instead to the Protestant Anglican Church that rejects the authority of the pope.

Cambridge University has a Protestant charter and almost all its teachers are Protestant. But James II is Catholic and wants to change things. He knows that the university is an important seat of power. He does everything he can to bring Catholic leaders to the university. But he's defeated. He's the last Catholic king of England.

NEWTON HELP US!

14. In Politics and Work

As I've said, I have my own ideas about religion. I studied the history of Christianity and I believe that today true Christians, bearers of the Truth, are rare, whether Catholic or Protestant.

But I have to keep that to myself. My century is a one of religious wars, where Christians slaughter and torture other Christians who believe in God in different ways. However, now I have to take sides and defend my university from the claims of King James. He wants to impose his men on the Cambridge staff. I think the university should be independent and managed by independent and politically neutral people. But that can only happen in a few centuries' time. Maybe.

CAMBRIDGE WILL REMAIN INDEPENDENT!

THE KING THREATENS OUR INDEPENDENCE!

With seven other teachers I go to London to defend the university. Our petition isn't taken very seriously, but during my visit there I meet many people and become friends with a man who will soon become important, the noble Charles Montague.

These are delicate years for my country. It's not just the independence of my university that's at stake. From Cambridge, and with some worry, I follow news of increased problems. A Dutch fleet sails up the Thames. Revolts break out everywhere. King James, oh so bravely, flees to France.

A new parliament gathers in Westminster and I'll be one of its members, elected by the academic senate of Cambridge. The new parliament proclaims two new rulers, William and Mary, but most important, it approves the Bill of Rights, which makes our country a freer one.

As for me, I decide to settle in the capital, the center of power for the whole nation. And immediately I'm given an important role.

THE KING HAS RUN AWAY!

HAIL TO THE NEW KING

BOOM BOOM BOOM

LONDON WILL BE MY CITY!

This is a cannon foundry in 1697. The coin factory, that is, the Mint of London, had much smaller furnaces and crucibles, but in terms of fire, smoke, and confusion, it wasn't far behind. At the time of Newton, coins were made of pure gold, silver, or copper. Most of these coins are subject to filing and endless forgery: only the newer coins are made by cutting them around their edges and inscribing the Latin words "Decus et tutamen," meaning "An ornament and a safeguard." These are the problems that Newton must face in his new job.

15. The "Clipping" of Coins

My friend Charles Montague gave me an unexpected and prestigious job: I'm the new inspector at the Mint of London. Here I can put my knowledge of alchemy and metallurgy to good use. I've been given a small apartment next to the Tower of London, overlooking the courtyard and the coin factory warehouses.

The mint is certainly not the best place to live. The noise starts early in the morning. Nearly 300 men work in very close quarters. Then there is the smoke from the forges, the noise of the soldiers, and horses that leave their dung in the courtyard, which is always, quite literally, covered in manure.

Neverthelesss, it's an important and strategic job for the kingdom of England. And then there's one curious aspect.

NO SCIENTIST IN HISTORY HAS EVER DEALT WITH SO MUCH MONEY!

My job at the mint has some very particular aspects. I have to swear not to give away the secrets of the machine that mints the coins.

I have to face a mountain of technical and administrative problems. I do it in a scientific way. I take notes on everything and everyone. I control the incoming raw materials and the quality of coins produced. In this way, I unmask a series of small and large crimes.

I improve the production and advise the government on how to fight counterfeiters and the strange practice of "clipping" old coins, which is when people file down the coins' edges to get gold and silver dust.

On my advice, the government passes a new law that makes counterfeiting a form of high treason. It becomes an offence punishable by death.

Among my duties I even have to interrogate the jailed counterfeiters. That's not a pleasant job. These criminals are skilled craftsmen, and they're as sneaky as the devil himself.

Between you and me, I always hope to meet someone who has discovered the secret sought by all alchemists: the formula to transform base metals into gold. Unfortunately, it never happens.

Here is William of Orange and his wife, Mary II, the new king and queen of England. Under their reign, Isaac Newton combines his friendships and his new position as a senior state official.

It's also the beginning of a period of greater peace and prosperity for England.

16. Newton's Life

I've changed a lot of my habits in London. In Cambridge, I led a sober and lonely life. Here, I have to visit parliament and I'm often invited to court. I spend a lot on expensive clothes and I get my portrait done by the major artists of my time. In fact, I'm collecting my portraits, where I insist that I'm given an aristocratic and majestic look.

In Cambridge, my favorite food was roasted quince, which is like a pear. I also have a cellar full of vintage wines and many other delicious things.

I receive awards and attention for my work at the mint and my recommendations to the government. I'm popular at court and among the aristocracy but also among the common people, who consider the laws I've discovered as supernatural.

If I can, I help my friends. For example, I get Edmond Halley the job of managing a branch of the mint.

My country house in Woolsthorpe is a distant memory. Now I live in a building with several floors in the center of London. My portraits decorate the walls of my house. The rooms are furnished with purple armchairs and sofas, crimson throws and curtains—everything around me is red and gold.

By the way, now I'm mature and well off, but I've never married. However, my house hosts an extraordinary feminine presence. She's my niece, the daughter of one of my half-sisters.

DO YOU LIKE MY HOUSE?

IT'S HIDEOUS!

She's the complete opposite of me: she's outgoing and has good taste. She once had smallpox, but luckily her face wasn't disfigured. Actually, she's beautiful and will become one of the most enchanting women in 18th-century London.

Here's Catherine Barton. Newton's beautiful niece is very popular in 18th-century London. She's at the heart of many rumors. The likable Jonathan Swift even dedicates an aching love poem to her.

A mysterious love story blossoms with the minister, Earl of Halifax, Charles Montague, a man of great power and an old friend of Newton's. Upon his death, the earl leaves a considerable estate to the young Catherine. Meanwhile, the earl helps Newton in his career, to the point that Voltaire, passing through London, insinuates that "his gravitation would've served no purpose without a beautiful niece."

In fact Newton, despite his temper, actually knows how to manage his public relations very well.

17. President of the Royal Society

HURRAH FOR PRESIDENT NEWTON!

THANK YOU THANK YOU

I volunteered to be president of the Royal Society. Up until now I preferred to stay away. It's falling apart and there are pointless meetings. Then finally that cheat, Hooke, dies. I have no more rivals in England.

I appoint a Curator of Experiments and conduct the first experiments on electricity. I immediately publish my studies on optics, which Hooke would have claimed as his own. Nobody complains. I'm the greatest British scientist now.

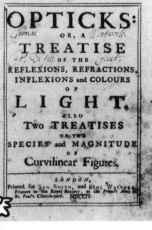

OPTICKS:

OR, A

TREATISE

OF THE

REFLEXIONS, REFRACTIONS, INFLEXIONS and COLOURS

OF

LIGHT.

ALSO

TWO TREATISES

OF THE

SPECIES and MAGNITUDE

OF

Curvilinear Figures.

LONDON,

Printed for SAM. SMITH, and BENJ. WALFORD, Printers to the Royal Society, at the Prince's Arms in St. Paul's Church-yard. MDCCIV.

IT'S ALL MY OWN WORK!

A scientific expedition to Finland proves that the Earth is flattened at the poles, as I predicted. My credibility and popularity as a scientist grows further.

Meanwhile, King William has died and on May 1, 1707, England and Scotland are joined in the United Kingdom of Great Britain. The new monarch is Anne, Mary's sister. I enjoy her respect and trust. In fact, she bestows me with the title of "Sir." I'm a knight.

In reality, I have many distinguished enemies and critics. The one I hate the most is Gottfried Wilhelm Leibniz, a German philosopher who claims to have invented one of the things I care most about.

In truth, Leibniz reached certain conclusions by himself, almost at the same time and without knowing about my work. But I'm merciless. I get him accused of plagiarism by the Royal Society and poor Leibniz dies without receiving any recognition for his many accomplishments.

Here's Isaac Newton in one of the countless portraits that he had made during his lifetime. He has always taken great care of his public image. He has become a powerful man, a "great man of science" as we would say today. He distributes favors to friends and thunderbolts to his enemies.

As the discoverer of the law of universal gravitation, he is destined to become a legend. He's considered a hero who uses theories instead of swords. He's respected by the nobility and very popular with Londoners. But he's also a very lonely man. He keeps terrible secrets and has opinions that many of his countrymen wouldn't share. He has always been honest and consistent, and he will be until the end.

18. The Last Night of Winter

In a few days it'll be spring, but I'm very sick.
Relatives, servants, and physicians flock to my house,
with its crimson chairs and purple velvet curtains.
They're all
very
worried.

I'm the man who discovered the laws that describe
the workings of the universe, the motion of the planets,
comets, and galaxies. But I'll not recover from the
complications of an ordinary gallstone.

I'm not complaining. I've never complained. But I
don't laugh either. I've laughed very little in my lifetime.
I've roared with laughter just once, when I was asked,
"What's the point in
reading Euclid's
Elements?"

On nights like this I can't help but think how strange my life has been.

I've been an extraordinary mathematician, but I've long kept hidden many of my findings. I'm considered the greatest scientist of my time, but like medieval magicians I tried to produce the philosopher's stone and the alchemic principle that would turn lead into gold. I searched for truth in ancient books and I kept the mysterious secrets I discovered to myself.

I never married and had no children, but I've always been surrounded by students and disciples, and I am comforted by an extraordinary niece.

I've always had a rather unsociable and dark character but I've always been respected by all. I've accumulated a remarkable fortune and will leave houses, land, and £30,000 in bonds ($11 million today) to my relatives.

But the biggest legacy I leave to mankind: my universal law. Not bad for the son of an illiterate farmer. Maybe this is the thing I'm most proud of.

Isaac Newton dies at age 84, on March 20, 1727. He leaves this world at around 1:00 in the morning, London time, due to a simple infection.

Newton's body was buried in Westminster Abbey after a lavish state funeral attended by the nobility of London and a huge crowd. The event was also witnessed by a great admirer of Newton's, the philosopher Voltaire.

A few years later, a grand monument was erected in Westminster Abbey at the expense of his relatives. On a bas-relief of the sarcophagus, two cherubs play with a prism, a telescope, and a map of the solar system. The epitaph reads, in Latin: "Mortals rejoice that there has existed such and so great an ornament of the human race."

Gravitational Dictionary

ABSOLUTE TIME

Newton believed that time was equal throughout the universe, but Albert Einstein later demonstrated that it's "relative." With respect to the Earth, for example, time slows down if we approach the speed of light. It slows down even if we approach a star or a big planet. There are places in the universe where time even stands still.

EVEN GENIUSES CAN MAKE MISTAKES!

ALCHEMY

This was the forerunner of modern chemistry. Its objective was the search for the legendary philosopher's stone and the transmutation of matter, such as changing lead into gold. Newton was one of the last great alchemists.

GOLD?

NO CHANCE!

FIZZZ!

GROAN!

ANTIGRAVITY FORMULA

Antigravity (in the title of this book) is nothing more than the opposite of gravitational force. The farther an object moves from a body or planet that attracts it, the weaker the force of attraction. The formula, or law, is therefore the same as the force of gravitation. It's not a magic formula but rather operates throughout the universe.

IT'S NOT A MAGIC FORMULA BUT . . . ALMOST.

$$F = G \frac{m_1 \cdot m_2}{r_2}$$

APPLE

The story of the apple has been told by several Newton biographers, especially by Voltaire. It's not certain that it really happened, but it's a great thought that such a big discovery was inspired by a falling fruit.

SIMPLE FRUIT . . . GREAT IDEA!

BLACK DEATH

The infectious microbe that caused it (*Yersina pestis*) takes its name from the Swiss doctor Alexandre Emile Jean Yersin, who isolated it in 1894. It infected humans and rats and was transmitted by the bite of fleas. The plague was defeated due to hygiene improvements in cities and the disappearance of the rats that spread it.

Not even the great Newton could have imagined this. However, when possible, he kept himself well away from the rats.

BOYLE, ROBERT

(1627–1691) He was an Irish naturalist and physicist. He's considered the founder of modern chemistry. He was skeptical about the mysterious practice of alchemy, but like Newton, he believed in the possibility of the transmutation of lead into gold . . .

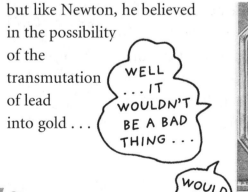

WELL . . . IT WOULDN'T BE A BAD THING . . .

WOULD IT?

ROBERTVS BOYLE NOBILIS ANGLVS

CAMBRIDGE

This is home to one of the most prestigious English universities. It was founded in 1209 by students and professors who had abandoned the equally prestigious Oxford University.

THERE WERE NO TOILETS, BUT IT WASN'T TOO BAD!

CAT DOOR

There's a strange story that claims Newton—during his experiments on light—made a hole in his front door to allow his cat to come and go as she pleased. When the cat had kittens, he made as many additional holes in the door as there were kittens.

THANKS, ISAAC!

CENTER OF GRAVITY

The gravitational force of a body attracts any surrounding bodies toward its center of gravity. For the Earth, it's the planet's core. But each body has its own center of gravity.

CENTRIFUGAL FORCE

This is the force that pushes outward in a body that is revolving. You can see it, for example, in a merry-go-round or the drum of a washing machine. The Earth also has some, as it revolves on its axis at a crazy speed. But the (centripetal) gravitational force is much stronger, so it keeps our feet firmly on the ground.

CENTRIPETAL FORCE

On Earth, this is the force of gravitation. "Centripetal" means "attracts toward the center." Newton came up with the name. It's a force that holds matter, the solar system, and the entire universe together.

CHARLES I

(1600–1649) The king of England who was beheaded in 1649. After him came the Puritan tyranny, led by the dictator Cromwell. Here he is in a famous portrait by the Flemish painter Antoon van Dyck.

CLIPPING OF COINS

This refers to the filing of the edges of gold and silver coins in order to obtain the precious dust of these metals, which was then melted down and sold. It

ceased to be an issue when an inscription to "safeguard" them was inscribed around the edge of the coins.

COMET

A celestial object that's composed mostly of ice, and which orbits our sun in a very long, elliptical circuit. The arrival of a comet, which seemed

amazing and unpredictable, was considered a bad omen.

COPERNICAN SYSTEM

This is the solar system as we now know it. It's also called a heliocentric system

because the sun (*Elios* in ancient Greek) is at its center and the planets revolve around it.

COPERNICUS, NICOLAUS

(1473–1543) He was the first "modern" astronomer to argue that the Earth revolves around the sun and not vice versa. In his time, this hypothesis was considered heretical. He proposed it in a book that was published only after his death—just in case.

YOU CAN NEVER BE TOO PRUDENT!

I DID THIS!

DRAWINGS

Newton drew freely and often. Drawing helped him to figure things out. This drawing, which shows Newton's experiment where he diffracts and recomposes light, was done by him.

DYNAMICS

This is the study of moving bodies
and the forces that move them.
Newton stated the three most
important laws of motion.

GROAN!

SPLAT!

EARTH'S SHAPE

The Earth is flattened at the poles and is wider at the
equator, where both the rotation speed and the
centrifugal force are
greater.

I'M A LITTLE ROUND AT THE MIDDLE. SO WHAT?

North

South

EINSTEIN, ALBERT

(1879–1955) Space and time were absolute values for Newton. But Einstein proved that time is relative and that in certain places in the universe, time can even stop.

ELLIPSE

In geometry, an ellipse is a set of points that have the same total distance from two fixed points known as "foci." You can draw an ellipse using a pencil and a string attached to the two points. The orbits of planets and comets are ellipses.

FLAMSTEED, JOHN

(1646–1719) He was the Astronomer Royal (director) of the Greenwich Royal Observatory. Newton took advantage of his position to get hold of the data from Flamsteed's observations.

JUST BETWEEN US: HE WAS A GREAT BULLY.

FORCE

This is what changes the shape, movement, expansion, attraction, and thrust of a body.

GALILEO GALILEI

(1564–1642) He was the first person to study and try to define gravity. He carried out some of his experiments on the Leaning Tower of Pisa.

THUD!

GRAVITATION

This is the most powerful force in the universe. It's the force that keeps the planets in their orbits around the sun. Nothing can stop it. Newton showed that this force attracts two bodies in proportion to their masses and inversely proportional to the square of the distance separating them.

GRAVITATIONAL ACCELERATION

Gravitational force accelerates the motion of any object falling toward the center of the Earth at the same rate (32 ft./sec^2 or 9.8 m/sec^2). In reality, air friction can counterbalance the force of gravity. So an object (or a parachutist) never exceeds a certain speed.

GRAVITY

The property of an object that makes it fall to the ground. It follows Newton's law of universal gravitation. Every body is attracted to the center of the Earth by a force proportional to its mass, and its main component is our planet's gravitational force of attraction. You want to measure this force? Just weigh the object.

GREENWICH

A suburb of London. It has been home to the famous observatory founded by Charles II since 1675. The meridian passing through Greenwich is considered the prime meridian at 0° longitude.

HALLEY'S COMET

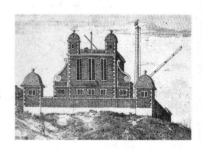

Thanks to Newton's formulas, Edmond Halley calculated the orbit of the comet that now bears his name. He was the first to predict its return, which happens on average every 75.3 years. The last time it appeared in the skies above the Earth was in 1986. The next visit is expected in 2061.

HOOKE, ROBERT

(1635–1702) He was an English naturalist, physicist, and inventor. He improved many instruments, including the microscope. He also invented the word "cell." He was Curator of Experiments at the Royal Society.

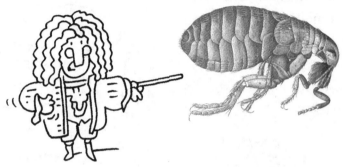

INERTIA

The tendency of a body to maintain its state of rest or motion. The measurement used to quantify it is mass.

KEPLER, JOHANNES

(1571–1630) He was a German astronomer. A staunch supporter of the ideas of Copernicus and Galileo, he discovered that the planets move around the sun in elliptical orbits.

LEIBNIZ, GOTTFRIED WILHELM

(1646–1716) He was a German mathematician and philosopher. Among other things, he designed one of the first mechanical calculators in history and suggested the use of the "binary system" that is now used in computer science. Independently from Newton, he also developed differential calculus. Newton accused him of plagiarism.

LIGHT

Today it's referred to as visible electromagnetic radiation. But for more than two centuries, Newton's theory that light was composed of particles was the one that prevailed.

MASS

Intuition tells us that the mass of a body is the "amount of matter" in it. In physics we can quantify it by using the relationship between the force applied to remove it from its state of inertia and the resulting acceleration.

MERCURY

A metal that was much loved by the alchemists. It has strange properties, mainly that it is a liquid at room temperature. It's very toxic. When Newton's hair was analyzed many years after his death, it was found to have 10 times the quantity of mercury that is considered tolerable.

WE DO THIS AND MORE FOR THE SAKE OF ALCHEMY!

MINT

This is a coin factory. The one in London was managed by Newton.

OPTICS

This is the study of light and the construction of instruments to improve vision.

ORBIT

This is the trajectory of a planet, comet, or artificial satellite around another celestial body. Newton's laws explain why all the orbits of the planets, comets, and even space debris tend to be elliptical.

PHOTONS

These are the "energy packets" that make up light. They have "particle" characteristics but are actually "packets" of electromagnetic waves.

PRISM

This is a transparent solid, typically made of glass, that's able to bend light, a phenomenon also known as refraction.

QUEEN ANNE

(1665–1714) Anne was crowned queen of England, Scotland, and Ireland on March 8, 1702. On May 1, 1707, England and Scotland were united into a single kingdom and Anne became the first monarch of the United Kingdom of Great Britain.

REFLECTING TELESCOPE

This was designed and built by Newton. It reflects and focuses the image, allowing for a greater sharpness.

REFLECTION

This happens when light rays encounter a surface and are bounced back toward the light source.

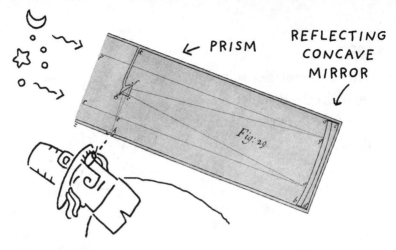

Fig. 29

REFRACTION

When light passes through a transparent body—a prism or water, for example—it's bent, or refracted. Here you can see how Newton took advantage of reflection and refraction to design his telescope. The drawing has been made by Newton himself.

SPECTRUM

Newton called it a spectrum because normally it can't be seen, just like the ghosts that haunt old houses. It's the group of different colors of electromagnetic radiation that compose a beam of light. In fact, even the natural phenomenon of the rainbow (created by microscopic droplets of water that refract and reflect light) makes it visible.

NOT A BAD
SPECTRUM!

SPEED

This is the relationship between the distance traveled and how long it took to get there.

TELESCOPE

Before the model designed by Newton, these were built longer and longer and larger, but with a very poor vision quality.

TIDES

This is the name given to the changing sea levels. They don't depend just on the Earth's centrifugal force and the gravitational pull of the sun and moon, but also on the depth of the seabed and the shape of the coastline. The result is that in certain places very fast-moving waves can occur, and they can be as high as 30 feet (10 meters).

UNIVERSE

By definition this is "everything that exists." But according to some modern physicists, there could be more than one universe . . .

VOLTAIRE

(1694–1778) He was a Parisian scholar, philosopher, and historian. He's one of the fathers of the Enlightenment. For several years he lived in exile in England, where he met Newton.

WEIGHT

This is the force of gravity acting on an object. The stronger the gravity, the heavier the object. Where there's no gravity, there's no weight.

WEIGHTLESSNESS

This is achieved by moving away from the Earth and its gravitational force.

LUCA NOVELLI

Writer, artist, journalist. He is
the author of books about
science and nature that have
been translated across the
world. He has collaborated with
the Italian television company, Rai, with WWF, and
with museums and universities. He wrote and
directed the "Lampi di Genio in TV" (Flashes of
Genius on TV) show for Rai Educational
(www.lampidigenio.it).

He won the Legambiente (League for the
Environment) award in 2001 and the Andersen Prize
for popularizing science in 2004.

FLASHES OF GENIUS

A series of biographies of the great scientists—all
written and illustrated by Luca Novelli—told in the
voice of the protagonist. It is a fun and engaging way
to approach science and to get to know the great
masters that changed the history of mankind. The
series won the Legambiente award in 2004.

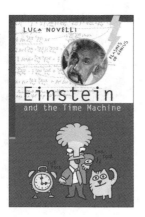

Einstein
and the Time Machine

Trade paper, 112 pages
ISBN: 978-1-61373-865-8
$9.99 (CAN $12.99)
Ages 7 to 10

Darwin
and the True Story of the Dinosaurs

Trade paper, 128 pages
ISBN: 978-1-61373-873-3
$9.99 (CAN $12.99)
Ages 7 to 10

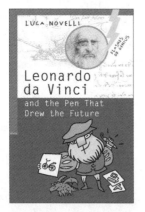

Leonardo da Vinci
and the Pen That Drew the Future

Trade paper, 112 pages
ISBN: 978-1-61373-869-6
$9.99 (CAN $12.99)
Ages 7 to 10